The Pareto Genealogical Records

Vittorio Emmanuel Pareto

2023

First published in 2020

Revised and updated on 5 January 2023

Copyright © Vittorio E. Pareto

ISBN: **9798648423466**

Printed in the USA by Amazon KDP
Cover: Victorio Emmanuel Pareto, the Genovese

Table of Contents

Table of Genealogical Charts

Introduction

This booklet presents the genealogical data of the Brazilian branch of the Pareto family. It is meant to be used as a general reference resource. The whole story of the Pareto family is told in another book: "A Family Tale," which includes this data.

These publications intend to satisfy a formal wish of my grandmother Hilda, who frequently requested her grandchildren to preserve the history of the family.

I am indebted to my cousins João Victorio Pareto Maciel, Vera Pareto d'Sá, and Paulo Henrique Gonçalves Monteiro for providing further data, updating information, and correcting errors, and to my son Vittorio Emmanuel Pareto for revising the manuscript.

This edition was revised in July 2022 to insert information retrieved from the inventory of Maria da Gloria Pareto and notes from João Victorio Pareto on his children and to update some branches.

Vittorio E. Pareto,
Aosta, July 2023.

Victorio Emmanuel Pareto, the Genoese.

The patriarch of the Pareto family branch in Brazil was **Vittorio Emmanuel Pareto**, born on 10 October 1818[1] in the town of Carrosio, Liguria, in the new Kingdom of Sardinia and Piedmont. Vittorio was the fifth son of Giovanni Battista Pareto and his wife, Antonia Chiappari.

Giovanni Battista, his father, was born in Carrosio on 14 September 1790[2], to Francesco Pareto and Geromima Cambiaso, both from San Quirico (Val Polcevera, Genova). Antonia Chiappari was a daughter of Lorenzo Chiappari.

Giovanni Battista and Antonia were married in Carrosio on 4 July 1811. They had seven children, all born and registered in Carrosio:

Maria Geronima (★9.07.1812),
Angela Maria (★7.09.1814),
Francesco Antonio Lorenzo (★14.06.1816),
Giuseppe (★2.08.1817),
Vittorio Emanuele (★10.10.1818 †6.09.1898),
Alessandro (★16.04.1820 †14.08.1823), and
Adamo (★20.08.1821).

Vittorio sailed from Genoa to Brazil in 1838, arriving in the port of Rio de Janeiro in March of the same year. In Brazil, Vittorio Emanuele was compelled to register using the name recorded in his baptism certificate, which was in Latin (*Victorius Emmanuel*). Since then, his name has become **Victorio Emmanuel Pareto,** which I will use here.

In Rio, Victorio Emmanuel started a relationship with Maria da Gloria Rapozo, born in 1826 in the parish of Santíssimo

[1] Book of Baptisms VI (1815-1837), Church of Santa Maria Assunta, Carrosio.
[2] Comune di Carrosio, 5th book of births, pg 176v.

Sacramento, Rio de Janeiro, daughter of the businessman José Joaquim Rapozo (†1849) and his wife, Áurea Benigna da Silva.

The couple had a daughter, Maria Antonia Pareto, born in Rio on 26 January 1843. On 5 Aug 1843 Victorio married Maria da Gloria in the Church of Candelaria[3]. They were the parents of six children[4]:

- Maria Antonia
- **João Victorio,**
- Francisca da Gloria,
- Maria da Gloria (Filha),
- Frederico Ernesto.
- Vittorio Emmanuel (Junior)

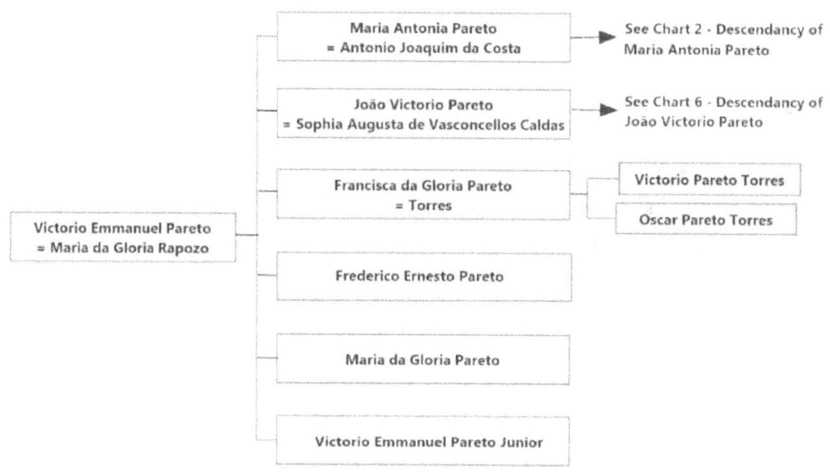

Figure 1 - Descendants of Victorio Emmanuel Pareto

[3] Book 10, pg. 55.
[4] When Maria da Gloria died (1893), Maria Augusta and her husband had already died and Francisca was a widow. All the other children were alive and living in the coffee plantation of Victorio Emmanuel, which was called "Santo Agostinho" and located in Conceição do Macabu, Macaé.

Maria da Gloria died on 13 May 1893 in Conceição do Macabu[5], Macaé, just after her 50th wedding anniversary. Vittorio Emmanuel died five years later, on 6 September 1898, in Rio de Janeiro. He was buried at the Cemetery of São Francisco Xavier[6].

Victorio Emmanuel has a place in Rio named in his memory: Travessa Victorio Emmanuel, in Tijuca.

[5] After the death af Maria da Gloria in 1893, Victorio Emmanuel moved to Rio (Rua Duque de Saxe, currently rua Pinheiro Machado).
[6] Also called Caju cemetery. On 2 June 1913, his grandson João Victorio Pareto Junior had his remains transferred to the São João Batista cemetery (tomb 2174) in Botafogo (Rio).

Maria Antonia and the Costa

Maria Antonia Pareto, the eldest child of Victorio Emmanuel and Maria da Gloria was born on 26 January 1843[7] and was baptized at the Church of Santíssimo Sacramento in Rio de Janeiro. In 1864 she married the lawyer Antonio Joaquim da Costa[i], delegate of Police in Macaé and colonel of the National Guard. Antonio Joaquim died in 1890, and Maria Antonia before 1893[8], in Macaé. They were the parents of twelve children[9], of which four did not leave offspring. Manuela and Maria Antoria died before 1893, probably while still infants. The children were:

- Mario Antonio,
- Octavio Antonio,
- Manuela,
- Hortencio Antonio,
- Tacito Antonio,
- Rolla Judith,
- Renato Antonio
- Manfredo Antonio,
- Horacio Antonio
- Helvécio Antonio,
- Maria Antonia and
- Manoela.

[7] Registro de Batismos da Paróquia do Santissimo Sacramento, book 1842-47 pg 138. Arquivo da Cúria Metropolitana do Rio de Janeiro.
[8] The remains of Antonio and Maria Augusta were transferred in 1906 from Macaé to the cemetery of SJB in Rio, tomb 2930.
[9] The genealogy of the descendants of Antonio Joaquim da Costa and Maria Antonia Pareto was provided by my cousin, Paulo Henrique Gonçalves Monteiro. The order of births of the children of Maria Antonia derived from the inventory of Maria da Gloria Pareto (1893).

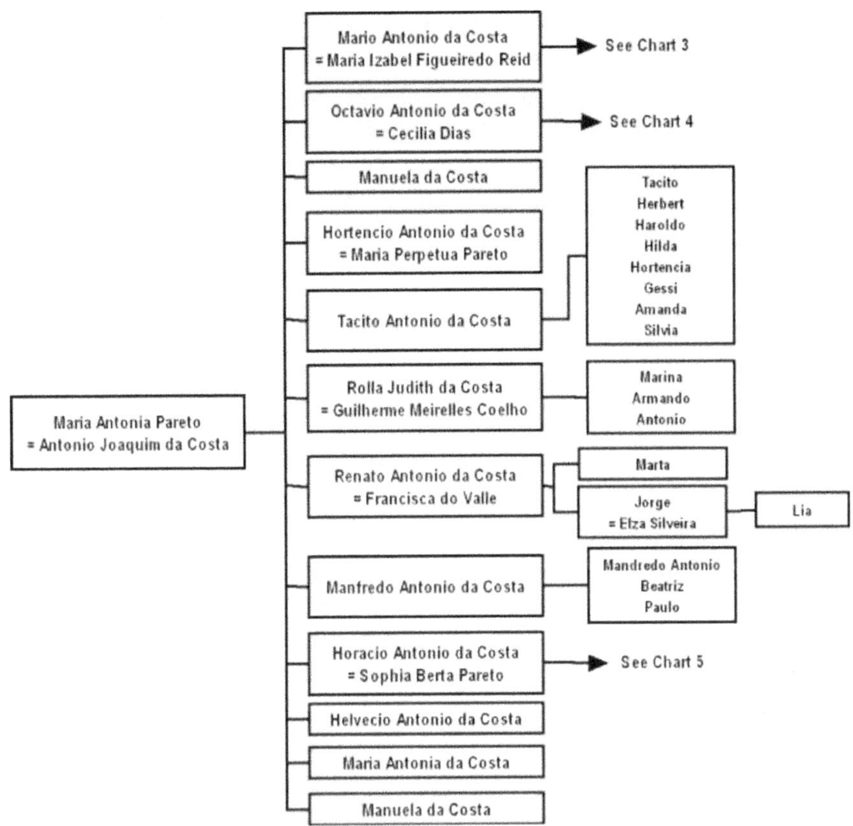

Figure 2 - Descendants of Maria Antonia Pareto

A. Mario Antonio da Costa[10] (vovô Coroca), was born on 10 August 1867 in Macaé and died on 25 July 1924. Lawyer in Macaé. He married Maria Izabel de Figueiredo Reid, born on 22 January 1873 in Conceição do Macabu, Macaé. Parents of:

    a. Afranio Antonio da Costa. Born on 14 March 1892, he died on 28 June 1979. Lawyer. Magistrate. Judge io Rio de Janeiro and (desembargador) and Federal Court of Appeals minister. He served in the Federal Supreme Court several times, replacing ministers. He was a Provider of the Santa Casa da Misericordia for 16 years.

[10] Buried at SJB at tomb 3030.

Afranio was the first Brazilian to win Olympic medals (Antwerp, 1920), winning silver and bronze medals[11]. He was married to Juracy Batista,

b. Soluta Reid da Costa was born on 25 Feb 1895. She died on 29 September 1966 in Rio. Married to Caio Julio Tavares (b. 1892 d. 1967) on 5 Feb 1892. Parents of:

    i. Heloisa Costa Tavares, married to Aristides Thibau Guimarães, parentes of:
        1. Carlos Augusto Thibau Guimarães
        2. Maria Lucia Thibau Guimarães

    ii. Maria Helena Costa Tavares, born in 1919. Married to Oscar Luiz Osorio Rheinganz, parents of:
        1. Marcia Tavares Rheinganz, married to José Rodrigues Gomes, parents of:
            a. Marina Gomes, married to Claudio Curi Hallal. Parents of:
                i. Bruna Hallal
            b. Isabel Gomes, married to Eduardo Mello. Parents of:
                i. Felipe Mello
                ii. Tomas Mello
            c. Otavio Rheinganz Gomes

[11] Afranio was the first Brazilian to win an Olympic medal, on 2 Aug 1920. A Brazilian won the gold medal, but on the following day.

2. Vera Tavares Rheinganz, married to Sergio Roberto Abuchaim. Parents of:
    a. Maria Rheinganz Abuchim, married to Alexandre Salvaterra. Parents of:
        i. Sergio Salvaterra
        ii. João Salvaterra
    b. Ricardo Rheinganz Abuchaim
    c. José Rheinganz Abuchaim, married to Fernanda Laranjeira. Parents of:
        i. Helena Abuchaim
    d. Pedro Abuchaim
3. Carlos Guilherme Rheinganz, married to Ligia Maria Silveira Rosa. Parents of:
    a. André Rheinganz, married to Sue Helen. Parents of:
        i. Marcelo Rheinganz
    b. Fernando Rheinganz
    c. Mário Rheinganz
4. Paulo Afonso Rheinganz, married to Ana Maria Silveira Lopes. Parents of:
    a. Gabriel Rheinganz
    b. Marcelo Rheinganz
5. Maria Gabriela Rheinganz, married to Carlos James Scainy. Parents of:
    a. João Luiz Scainy
    b. Carolina Scainy

iii.

Maria Amelia Costa Tavares, married to Pedro Nolasco Canto. Parents of
1. João Batista Canto
2. Sofia Helena Canto
3. Pedro Canto
4. Maria Amelia Canto
5. Maria Isabel Canto
6. Julio Canto

  iv. Silvia Costa Tavares, married to Luiz Amaral. Parents of:
1. Angela Amaral
2. Luiz Alexandre Amaral
3. Luiz Guilherme Amaral
4. Luiz Eduardo Amaral
  v. Mario Costa Tavares.
c. Maria Antonia Reid da Costa, without offspring.

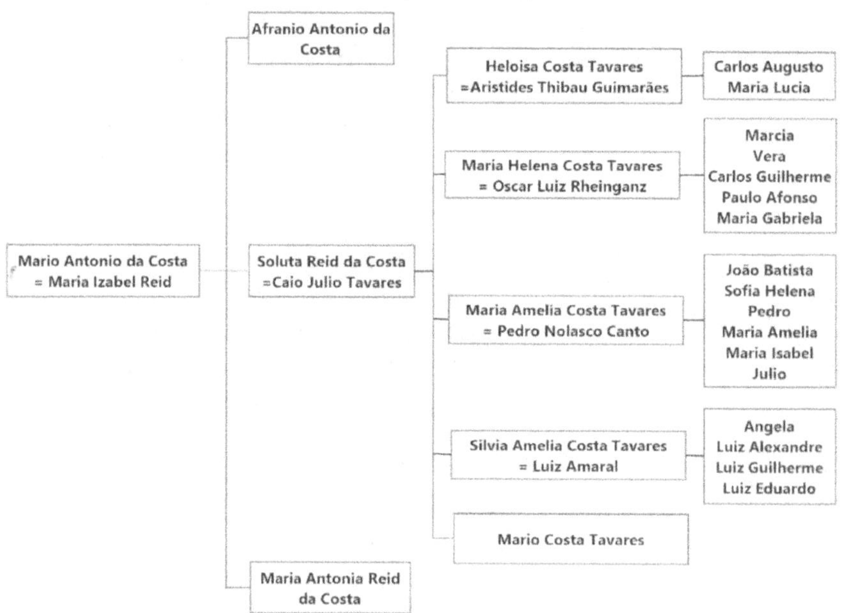

Figure 3 - Descendants of Mario Antonio da Costa

B. Octavio Antonio da Costa[12], born in Macaé, died on 6 November 1940. Public Attorney in Macaé and judge in Cantagalo, Niteroi, and Rio. Desembargador of the Rio de Janeiro's Court of Appeals. In 1892 he married Cecilia Dias[13] (d. 5 December 1949). Parents of:

    a. Onila da Costa born on 4 Sept 1893 and died on 28 Aug 1965. Married Cicero Monteiro[14] on 28 Dec 1912. Parents of:

        i. José da Costa Monteiro, married to Luiza Alves da Silveira. Parents of:

            1. Luiz Fernando da Silveira Monteiro

            2. Lucia Helena Monteiro, married to Helio Borges. Parents of:

                a. João Luiz Borges

                b. André Borges, married to Aécia. Parents of;

                    i. Bruna Borges

                c. Priscila Borges

        ii. Thelio da Costa Monteiro born on 25 Sept 1914. Lawyer and delegate of the Police in São Paulo. Magistrate. Minister and president of the São Paulo and Rio de Janeiro labor courts. Minister and president of the Federal Labor Higher Court in Brasilia. Thelio married twice. With Elizabeth Salles (★13 Nov 1920), he was the father of:

            1. Carlos Henrique Salles Monteiro, born on 12 June 1939, died 15 May 2007. Married three times. First to Vangi Gonçalves Ferreira (= 3 Oct 1963), born 29 Aug 1942). Parents of:

---

[12] Octavio died on 7 November 1940 and was buried at the SJB cemetery tomb 2930.

[13] Daughter of Antonio Caetano Dias, one of the founders of the town of Macaé, and his wife Eliza Gonçalves Dias.

[14] Cicero was born on 26 April 1885 in Leopoldina, MG, son of Martiniano de Souza Monteiro and Estephania Ferreira de Castro. Cicero died of cancer on 18 December 1972.

a. Paulo Henrique Gonçalves Monteiro, MBA. born on 24 November 1964) married to Rosangela de Oliveira Pinto (★20 Mar 1973 =22 Mar 1997). Parents of:
   i. Bruna Constanze de Oliveira Monteiro, born on 22 February 2002.
   ii. Sophia Helena de Oliveira Monteiro, born on 24 November 2006 in São Paulo.
b. Teresa Cristina Gonçalves Monteiro born on 14 Jan 1966. Married to Marcio Ungerer, having a son:
   i. Rafael Gonçalves Ungerer, born on 21 September 1989.
   Teresa married again to Vanderlei Spedini, having a daughter:
   ii. Mariana Spedini born on 20 Feb 1996.
c. Flavio Roberto Gonçalves Monteiro, born 17 December 1968), married to Maria Teresa Abboud, having a son:
   i. Kalil Monteiro
The second wife of Carlos Henrique was Elizabeth Mendes (★5 Dec 1948), with whom he had a daughter:
d. Fernanda Mendes Monteiro, married to Marcos (?), with a daughter:
   i. Beatriz.

Carlos Henrique third wife was Ruth de Souza(★8 Mar 1952), with whom he had a son:

> e. Carlos Alexandre Souza Monteiro.

2. Paulo Roberto Salles Monteiro, born 10 September 1945. Married to Marilena Sernache (★22 July 1947). Parents of:

> a. Cynthia Sernache Monteiro born on 8 Feb 1973. Married to Luiz Felipe de Lamare Fonseca. Parents of:
>
>> i. Gabriella Fonseca, born on 20 March 2004.
>>
>> ii. Isabella Fonseca
>
> b. Felipe Sernache Monteiro, lawyer. Born on 14 March 1975.

Thelio's second wife was Regina Maria da Costa, with whom he was the father of:

3. Thelio Mario da Costa Monteiro, who married twice:

With Dulce von Müller Thome Torres he had a son:

> a. Gabriel.

With Michelle Souzuet, he had another son:

> b. Michel.

iii. Alino da Costa Monteiro, lawyer. Born on 23 January 1916. She died in Brasilia. Married to Evany Catharina Rodrigues dos Santos[15]. Parents of:

1. Maria Cecilia da Costa Monteiro, born 9 March 1964). Married to Bernd Peter Wansart[16]. Parents of:

[15] Born in the island of Paquetá, Rio.
[16] From Koln, Germany.

        a. Bernd Peter Monteiro Wansart, born on 2 May 1986 in São Paulo.

b. Odir da Costa, married to Rosa Guillobel. He died on 3 May 1951 and was buried at the São João Batista cemetery in Rio, tomb 2930. Parents of:
    i. Paulo Guillobel da Costa
    ii. Helda Guillobel da Costa, married to Manoel (?). Parents of
        1. Eduardo
        2. Fernando, married to Beatriz with one son:
            a. Olavo
        3. Ricardo
    iii. Helena Guillobel da Costa, married to Hermano Ribenboim (d. 2004). Parents of:
        1. Miriam,
        2. Paulo Arthur,
        3. José Carlos.

c. Mario Dias da Costa, physician. Married to Maria Amalia Montenegro. Parents of:
    i. Elio da Costa, born in Jau, SP.
    ii. Ione Montenegro da Costa
    iii. Roberto da Costa

d. Maria Antonia Dias da Costa, died 7 June 1965.

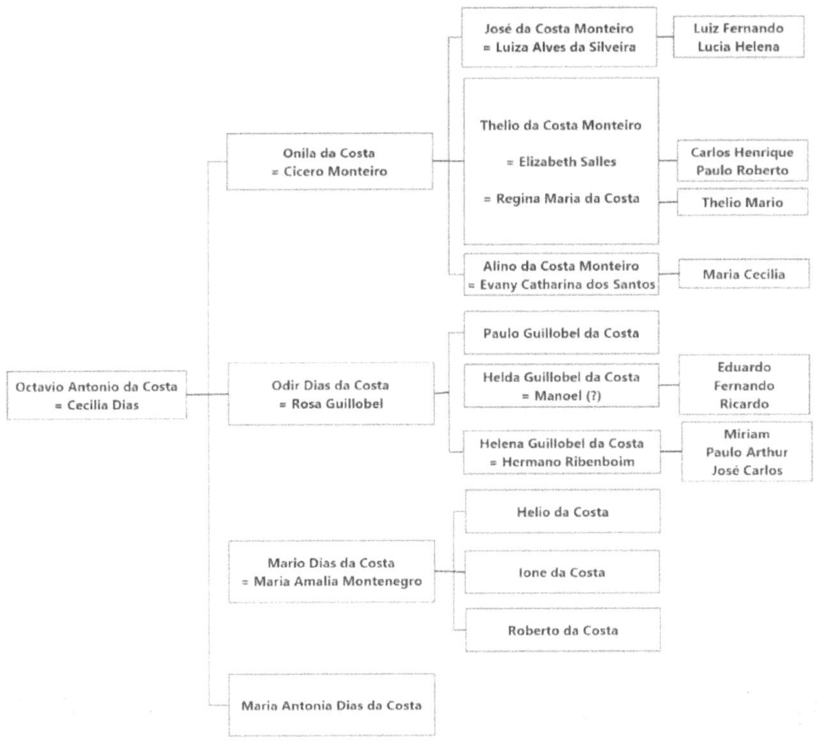

Figure 4 - Descendants of Octavio Antonio da Costa

C. Manuela da Costa (died infant).

D. Hortencio Antonio da Costa married his cousin Maria Perpetua Pareto (daughter of João Victorio Pareto), yet he died without offspring on 12 March 1907. Maria Perpetua married again and had offspring (see the genealogy of João Victorio Pareto). He was buried in the SJB cemetery in Rio, tomb 2930.

E. Tácito Antonio da Costa, married Amanda, from England.
Parents of:
   a. Tacito da Costa Filho
   b. Herbert da Costa
   c. Haroldo da Costa
   d. Hilda da Costa
   e. Hortencia da Costa
   f. Gessi da Costa
   g. Amanda da Costa
   h. Silvia da Costa

F. Rolla Judith da Costa married the physician Guilherme
Meirelles Coelho. She was buried at the São João Batista
cemetery, tomb 2930. Parents of:
   a. Marina
   b. Armando
   c. Antonio

G. Renato Antonio da Costa, born in 1875. Married to Francisca
do Valle (Franchita). Parents of:
   a. Marta da Costa
   b. Jorge do Valle Costa, born on 28 August 1907. Married
       to Elza Silveira. Parents of:
          i. Lia Silveira da Costa

H. Manfredo Antonio da Costa born on 24 Feb 1876. Engineer.
Participated in the São Paulo revolution of 1932 against Getulio
Vargas and was elected to the constitutional assembly of São
Paulo in 1934. He died on 11 April 1957. Father of:
   a. Manfredo Antonio da Costa Filho
   b. Beatriz da Costa
   c. Paulo da Costa

I. Horácio Antonio da Costa was born on 28 January 1878.
Engineer. General Inspector of the Mogiana Railways (SP). The
municipal stadium of Campinas is named after him, and his bust
in bronze is placed at the entrance. He married his first cousin
Sophia Berta Pareto (daughter of João Victorio Pareto), born
on 29 January 1883. Parents of:

a. Sophia Helena da Costa. Married Oscar Figueiredo. She died at 22, giving birth to a daughter:

    i. Sophia Helena Figueiredo. She married the lawyer José Vicente, who died in a car accident in 1980. Parents of:

        a. Berta Maria Vicente. Married with three children.

        b. Sophia Helena Vicente. Married with four children.

        c. Solange Vicente. Married with one daughter.

        d. Fernando Antonio Vicente. Married with three children.

        e. Emilia Vicente, married.

        f. Angela Vicente.

        g. João Batista Vicente

        h. Suzana Vicente. She died with her father in an accident (1980).

b. Horácio Antonio da Costa Filho. Married Lucia Siqueira Soares. Parents of:

    i. Lucia Maria da Costa. Married with four children.

    ii. Alda Maria da Costa. Married with three children.

    iii. Horacio Antonio da Costa, married.

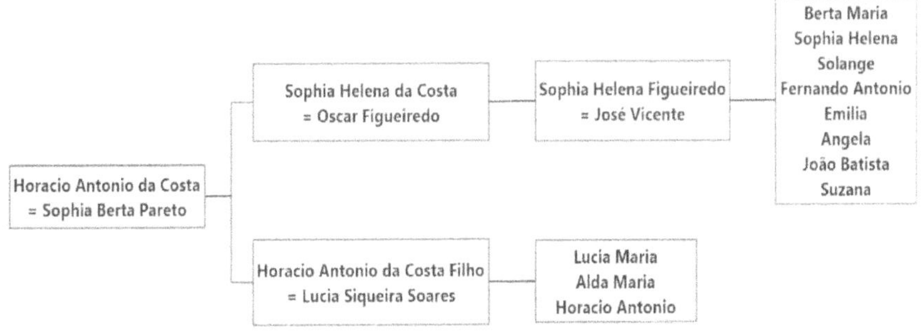

Figure 5 - Descendants of Horacio Antonio da Costa and Sophia Berta Pareto

J. Helvécio Antonio da Costa, born in 1879. He died in São Paulo before 1924 but was buried in Rio on 11 February 1924 at the São João Baptista cemetery, tomb 2930.

K. Maria Antonia da Costa. She died before 1893. Buried on 1 July 1965 in the São João Baptista cemetery, tomb 2930, and

L. Manuela da Costa died infant, as her homonymous sister.

Dr. João Victorio Pareto, the magistrate.

João Victorio Pareto, the second child of Victorio Emmanuel, was born on 25 March 1845 in Rio de Janeiro and was baptized on 25 March 1846[17] at the Church of Santissimo Sacramento. In Rio de Janeiro, he was a magistrate and state representative (second and third legislatures). He married Sophia Augusta de Vasconcellos Caldas on 17 October 1878 in Macaé[18]. Sophia was born on 17 September 1860 in the town of Miranda[19], province of Mato Grosso do Sul, daughter of the magistrate Dr. José Caldas and Guilhermina Maria da Conceição de Vasconcellos.

João Victorio and Sophia had ten children: Maria Perpétua, João Victorio Junior, Sophia Berta, Flavio José, Afranio, José, Ofisa, Andréa, and the twins Raul Carlos and Carlos Raul[20].

João died on 17 February 1919 in Rio de Janeiro and was buried in the cemetery of São João Batista, in the same tomb where his father, Vittorio Emmanuel, his wife Sophia, and his sister Francisca da Gloria also rest[21]. Sophia Augusta died on 1 February 1934 in Rio de Janeiro.

João Victorio has a school and a street named after him in Rio. The street Santa Sophia in Rio is named after his wife, Sophia Augusta.

[17] Registry of Baptisms of the Church of Santissimo Sacramento, book 1842-1847 pg 233v – Arquivo da Cúria Metropolitana do Rio de Janeiro.
[18] Marriage Records, Book 4, pg 28v. Church of São João Batista, Macaé.
[19] Miranda was then a small village. It was destroyed during the war with Paraguay (1864-1870), probably the reason for family returning to Rio.
[20] Sophia Augusta had a miscarriage on 24 May 1894 in Lambary, Minas Gerais. The girl died shortly after birth and was not given a name.
[21] Tomb 2174.

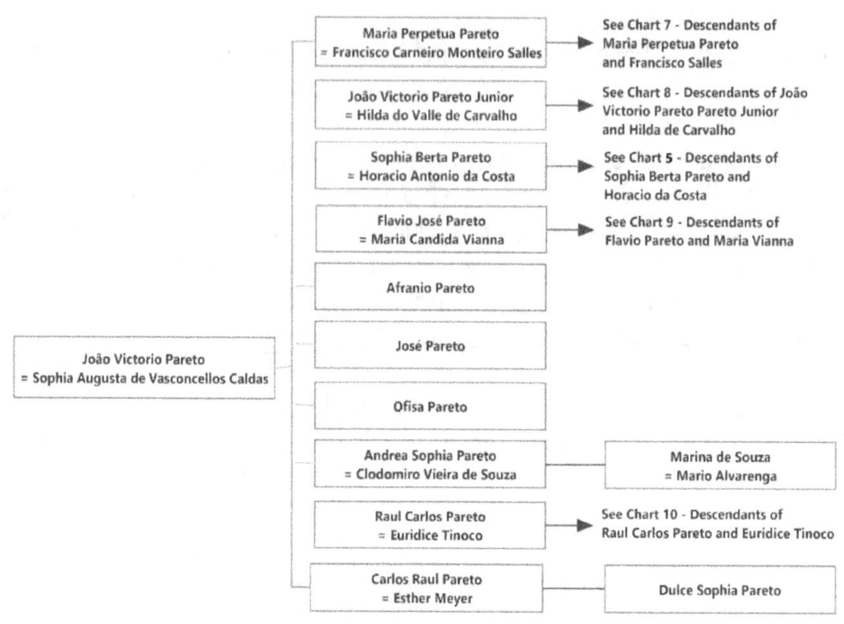

Figure 6 - Descendants of João Victorio Pareto

A. Maria Perpétua Pareto (tia Zinha) born on 12 September 1879[22]. She married her first cousin, Hortêncio Antonio da Costa, who died before they had children.

She married a second time to the lawyer Francisco Carneiro Monteiro de Salles. Parents of:

    a. Francisco Monteiro de Salles. Married Carmem Silva e Souza. He died in 1989. Parents of:

        i. Lilia Monteiro de Salles. Married Hélcio Navarro Serpa. Parents of:

            1. Marcello Helvecio Serpa. Married to Monica Morel.

            2. Renata Serpa. Married to Ricardo José Medina Barbosa.

            3. Fabio Serpa.

Francisco married a second time to Yolanda Jacovino, having a son:

        ii. Francisco Monteiro de Salles. Married, without children.

    b. Elisa Maria Monteiro de Salles. Married the ophthalmologist José Luiz Novaes. Parents of:

        i. Eduardo de Salles Novaes. Married to Leah Mary Gray, having two daughters:

            1. Leah Novaes

            2. Luiza Maria Novaes, married to Fabian de Gropallo.

Eduardo married a second time to Junia de Vilhena, having another daughter:

            3. Joana Novaes.

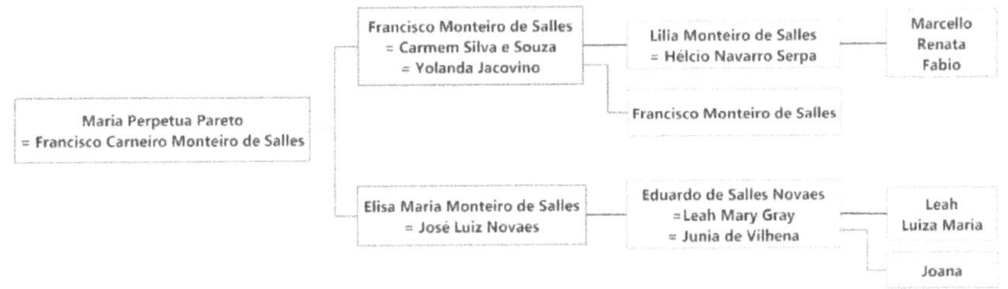

Figure 7 - Descendants of Maria Perpetua Pareto

[22] At his house at Praia do Flamengo 50.

B. **João Victorio Pareto Junior, the Lawyer.** João was born on 14 October 1880 in Macaé at his home in Rua Direta, corner with Rua Barão de Cotegipe[23]. He graduated in Law in 1902 and married Hilda do Valle de Carvalho on 14 October 1903[24]. Hilda was born on 1 May 1885 in Cantagalo, RJ[25], daughter of Senator Miguel Joaquim Ribeiro de Carvalho and Izabel do Valle and granddaughter of the Portuguese nobleman João Maria do Valle. João Victorio and Hilda had five children: Maria Carmem, João Victorio Pareto Netto, Victorio Emmanuel, Luiz Henrique, and Maria Lucia. João Victorio Pareto Junior died on 31 July 1937 in Rio and was buried at São João Batista's cemetery[26]. Hilda died on 13 July 1983, being buried next to her husband. She has a place in Rio named after her, the Praça Hilda, in Tijuca. They were the parents of:

   a. Maria Carmem Pareto was born on 7 August 1904 at Rua Capitão Salomão 15. She was baptized on 1 May 1905 at the church of Largo do Machado. She married the journalist José Soares Maciel Filho (★25.12.1903 † 21.01.1975) on 4 January 1930). Maciel Filho was a personal friend of President Vargas and is reputed to have written his political will. He was the first president of the National Development Bank (BNDE) and superintendent of SUMOC, which would become the Brazilian Central Bank. Maria Carmem died on 2 Feb 1982. Parents of:

   i. Hilda Pareto Maciel born on 27 Dec 1930[27] in Rio de Janeiro and died on 25 Feb 2007. She married the physician Antonio Luiz de Medina. Parents of:

   1. Antonio Luiz de Medina born on 14 Oct 1953. Married to Heloisa Vasconcellos. Parents of:

---

23 All the children of João Victorio born in the town of Macaé were born in his house in Rua Direita, corner of Rua Barão de Cotegipe.
24 Church of Candelaria, register of Marriages, Book 12 pg 113.
25 Church of Santissimo Sacramento, Cantagalo (RJ).
26 Tomb 2173.
27 Hilda was born at Praia do Russell 180, in Rio.

a. Joana Maria de Medina, born on 19 Mar 1976,

b. João Inacio de Medina, born on 25 November 1979 and

c. Juliana de Medina born on 2 Dec 1982.

2. Antonio José de Medina. Single.

Hilda married a second time to José Carlos Lisboa, having one more son:

1. José Carlos Lisboa, born on 30 August 1967. He lives in Sao Paulo.

ii. Maria Isabel Pareto Maciel. Born on 10 August 1932 in Rio de Janeiro and died in 2011 in Petropolis. She married the lawyer and industrialist Marcello Veloso Borges from Paraiba. Parents of:

1. Priscila Veloso Borges. Married Jacques Guesgorin. Parents of:

a. Chaim Guesgorian (Fogo) is married to Heloisa Soares and has a daughter, Sofia.

Priscila had a relationship with Edison, having a daughter:

b. Violeta is married to Jean Paul Stoyanov and has a daughter, Clara.

Priscilla had a relationship with Luiz Freire and had a son:

c. Luiz, married to Isenschmid, having two children: Camilla and Victor;

Priscilla is married to Damien Bugmann and lives in Bienne, Switzerland.

2. Marcello Veloso Borges (Marcelinho), married.

3. Izabel Veloso Borges (Bebel). Had a daughter from a relationship:

a. Carolina.

iii. José Soares Maciel, born on 30 March 1934 in Petropolis and died on 5 August 2013. Married Sonia Lucia Possolo. Parents of:

    1. José Soares Maciel, born on 16 August 1958. Married to Princia de Souza Marinho, born on 26 November 1964. Parents of:

        a. Antonio Pedro Marinho Soares Maciel born on 18 Feb 2002.

iv. João Victorio Pareto Maciel, born on 3 January 1942[28] in Rio and died on 6 April 2021. Married Angela Rodrigues. Parents of:

    1. João Victorio Pareto Maciel, born on 7 April 1973.

    2. Livia Pareto Maciel, born on 8 May 1979. Architect.

b. João Victorio Pareto Netto, born on 17 December 1905 at Rua Marques de Abrantes 126[29]. Baptized on 1st May 1906 at the church of N.S. Gloria. Engineer. Married on 16 February 1932 Heloisa Bastos de Oliveira (★11.04.1907 †29.10.1985) in Petropolis (tia Lulú). Died on 15 November 1979. Parents of:

i. Gilda Bastos de Oliveira Pareto, born on 17 September 1934 in Rio. Architect, single.

ii. João Carlos Pareto was born in July 1937 in Rio and died on 18 April 2000 of bone cancer. Engineer. Married to Thereza Silva Pereira. Parents of:

    1. João Carlos Pareto Junior, born on 19 Feb 1965. Married Rosilene Portela. Parents of:

        a. Juliana Portela Pareto, born on April 1994. Married on 22 September 2018 to Artur Koatz Gurvitz.

---

[28] João Victorio Pareto Maciel was born at Praia do Russell 180 in Rio.
[29] The villa of his maternal grandfather, senator Miguel de Carvalho Jr.

b. Fernanda Portela Pareto, born on 29 April 1996

2. Eduardo Luiz Pareto, born on 9 July 1969. Married to Flavia Magalhães. Parents of:

    a. Beatriz, born on 2 Oct 2002.

    b. Julia, born on 9 Oct 2004.

João Carlos (father) married a second time to Heliana Machado Mendonça. Parents of:

3. Daniel Mendonça Pareto, lawyer, married Gisele Xavier on 30 September 2006, with one daughter:

    a. Catarina born on 5 Jan 2011 in Rio de Janeiro.

iii. Vera Pareto. Born on 4 March 1951 in Rio. Economist. Married the engineer Cedric d' Sá, from Karachi, Pakistan. Parents of:

1. Heloisa Pareto de Sá, born 30 August 1984, married to David Jorge Kaddoum with a daughter:

    a. Isabel de Sá Kaddoum, born on 1st March 2018.

2. Mario Caetano Pareto de Sá, born on 4 August 1989, married Isabela in 2022.

c. **Victorio Emmanuel Pareto,** born on 24 March 1913[30] at Rua Senador Vergueiro 167.   Lawyer. He was baptized at the Church of Candelaria on 14 October 1913 and died on 15 June 1999. He married on 22 January 1936 Maria Picorelli[31] (★Porto Alegre, 21.05.1912 †17.04.1956), daughter of Dr. José Picorelli and Morena Bica, at the Church of Sta. Terezinha[32] in Rio. Parents of:

> i. **Vittorio Emmanuel Pareto Junior**[33] born on 9 May 1937[34] in Rio de Janeiro. Baptized at the São Bento Monastery on 24 March 1938[35]. Architect. Doctor in urban development[36] and other academic titles. Married to Alba Maria Madalena Lerche Pompeu (★Fortaleza, 25. 09.1937), daughter of the entrepreneur Thomas Pompeu de Souza Brasil Netto[37] and Birthe Flagstad Lerche[38] on 19 December 1959[39] and at the Church of Sta. Maria Maria da Lagoa on 21 January 1960[40]. He lives in Aosta, Italy. Parents of:
>
> > 1. **Vittorio Emmanuel Pareto** was born on 17 December 1960 in Rio de Janeiro[41] and baptized at the Monastery of São

---

[30] Cartorio 4 Oficio. Book 109, pg 24v. Register 470.

[31] Cartorio 5 Oficio, Book 74 pg 63 Register 95. Maria spoke fluently French and English. She studied art in London and Paris and was awarded bronze and silver medals at the National Fine Art Exibition (1953).

[32] Parish of S. João Batista da Lagoa, Book 16 pg 112.

[33] The Junior suffix was removed from his name in Italy and in the USA.

[34] Cartório 4 Oficio, Book 211 pg 50v.

[35] Baptism Register, Book 1 pg 39.

[36] University College London, Feb 1983.

[37] Was president of the Brazilian Confederation of Industries. Knight of Order of Infant D. Henrique (Portugal).

[38] Born in Copenhagen, Denmark

[39] Cartorio 5 Oficio, Book B162 pg 232, register 21209.

[40] Marriages Register, Book 3 pg 105.

[41] Cartorio 5 Oficio, Book 444 pg 30v, register 122073.

Bento[42]. Doctor in nuclear engineering (MIT) and MBA[43]. Married on 30 December 1989 to the physician Gail Lynn Ellis (★Lakeview, OH 18.01.1967), daughter of Russell Ellis and Janet Wagner. Parents of:

    a. Alexander Wagner Pareto was born on 16 March 1997 in Beverly, MA. Software engineer (USC)

    b. Henry Gordon Pareto was born on 12 October 1999 in Beverly (MA). Psychologist (UMass).

2. Otto Pompeu Pareto, born on 1 July 1978[44] in Brasilia. Graduated in Hospitality[45] and has an MBA[46]. Married to Chie Matsumoto[47] on 6 April 2001 in London, Daughter of Senji Matsumoto and Ayako Matsumoto. Parents of:

    a. Kaya Maria Vittoria, born on 17 January 2005 in Aosta, Italy.

    b. Gianluca Kentaro Raffaele, born on 17 March 2008 in Rio de Janeiro, Brazil.

From a union with Nayeku Arenas Orozco, he has a daughter:

    c. Lea Francesca Pareto Arenas, born on 23 January 2021 in Cancun, Mexico.

3. Marcos Pompeu Pareto. Born on 28 November 1980[48] in Brasilia. Master in Economics[49]. Single.

---

[42] Baptism Register Book 5 pg 97 register 778
[43] Tutored by the Nobel laureate Franco Modigliani (MIT, Sloane School).
[44] Cartorio 1 Oficio, Book 79, pg 440 Register 46640.
[45] Middlesex University London.
[46] Getulio Vargas Foundation.
[47] Born in Hagi, Yamagushi (Japan)

ii. Marcos Eduardo Pareto born on 21 Jul 1945. He married on 5 September 1979 Sonia Maria Cardoso de Oliveira, born on 4 May 1947. He died of cancer on 23 June 2011 in Rio[50]. Parents of:

1. Maria Elisa Pareto born on 1 Dec 1971 in Rio. She died on 2 September 2019.
2. Luiz Eduardo Pareto, born 11 September 1975 in Rio, sociologist. Married on 3 Jun 2009 to Luzia Milione, born 13 Dec 1973. Parents of:
   a. Beatriz.

Victorio Emmanuel, widowed in 1956, married a second time in 1958 to Clarita Prestes de Oliveira from Cruz Alta, RGS. Parents of:

iii. João Victorio Pareto, born 10 November 1960 in Rio de Janeiro, married Lucy Ann Aparecida Bahanan Knezevic without offspring.

d. Luiz Henrique de Carvalho Pareto, born on 16 December 1914 at Rua Sen. Vergueiro 167, Rio, was baptized at the Church of Candelária on 14 October 1915. He died on 6 September 2006 in Rio. Lawyer. Married Seli de Lourdes Bueno (tia De Lourdes), from Rio Grande do Sul (★08.05.1915 †08.05.1971). Parents of:

i. Anna Maria Pareto, born on 7 Oct 1937 in Rio. Married Carlos Alberto de Abreu in 1958. Parents of:

1. Carlos Alberto de Abreu Junior (Bebeto), born on 15 January 1960 in Rio. Lawyer, single.
2. Luiz Henrique Pareto de Abreu (Guingo), born on 11 May 1961 in Rio, single.

---

[48] Cartorio 1 Oficio, Book 79, pg 440 Register 46641.
[49] Graduated at UMass. Master of Economics, Boston University.
[50] Book C-00288, pg 026, Register 78516.

Divorced in 1967, Anna Maria married Ítalo Mencoboni from Pesaro, Italy in 1978. Parents of a daughter:

3. Rafaella Pareto Mencoboni. Lawyer. Born on 15 August 1978 in Rio, married to Carlos Alexandre Rangel Guimarães. Parents of:

   a. Ana Luiza Pareto Mencoboni Guimarães, born on 26 Janeiro 2006.

   b. Luiz Felipe.

e. Maria Lucia Pareto, the last child of João Victorio and Hilda, was born in 1915 and died with only 25 days of life[51]. She was buried at the cemetery of São João Batista with her parents[52].

[51] The autopsy revealed that she has had swallowed a copper thimble that oxidized in her stomach and poisoned her.
[52] Cript 2173.

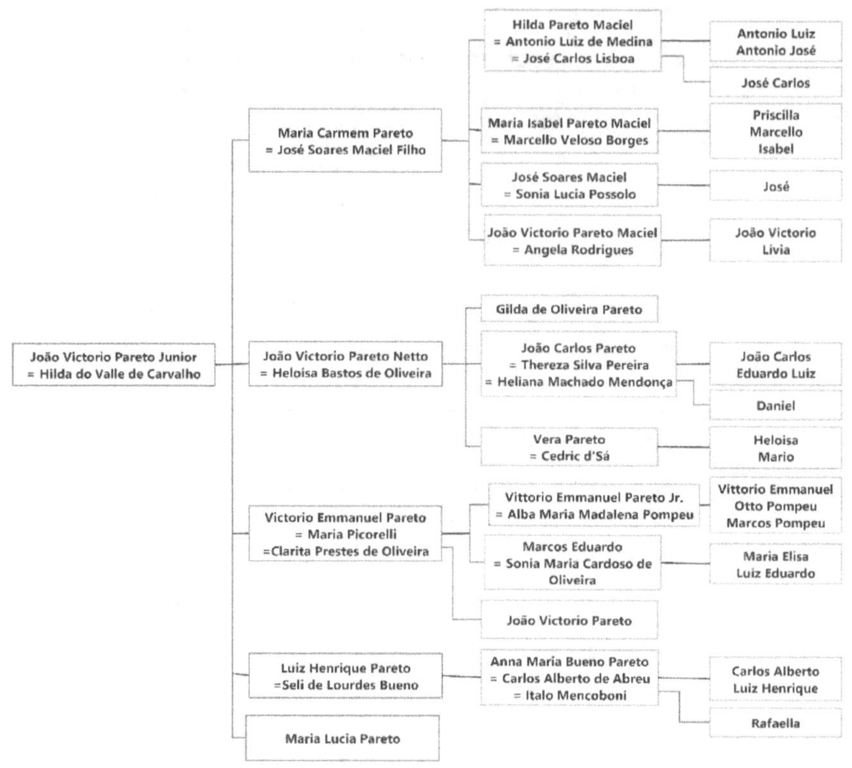

Figure 8 - Descendants of João Victorio Pareto Jr.

C. Sophia Berta Pareto born on 21 Jan 1883 in Macaé. She was baptized on 29 July 1884[53] and married her first cousin, the engineer Horacio Antonio da Costa, son of Maria Antonia Pareto and Antonio Joaquim da Costa. They had two children: Sophia Helena and Horacio da Costa Filho, with offspring.
Her descendancy is listed under her husband, Horacio Antonio da Costa (chart 5).

D. Flavio José Pareto (tio Flavio). Born on 29 July 1884 in Macaé. Married Maria Candida Vianna in 1908. Parents of:

[53] Baptism Register, Book 4 pg 65. Church São João Batista, Macaé.

a. Maria de Lourdes Pareto (Mariazinha). Married Aguinaldo Perdigão. Parents of:
   i. Maguy Perdigão
   ii. Aguinaldo Perdigão, married to Miriam Curi. Parents of:
      1. Monica Perdigão
      2. Henrique Perdigão
      3. Marcelo Perdigão
      4. Simone Perdigão
      5. Bernardo Perdigão, deceased.
b. Flavio José Pareto (Flavinho), born on 21 Mar 1910, died on 22 Oct 1989. He married Martha Mourão Russell in 1933. Parents of:
   i. Martha Maria Pareto, married to Renato Pontes.
   ii. Noemi Pareto, married to José Conrado. Parents of:
      1. Flavia Conrado
      2. João Frederico Conrado
c. Ophisa Pareto, married to Eduardo Duvivier. She died at 21, giving birth. The child also died.

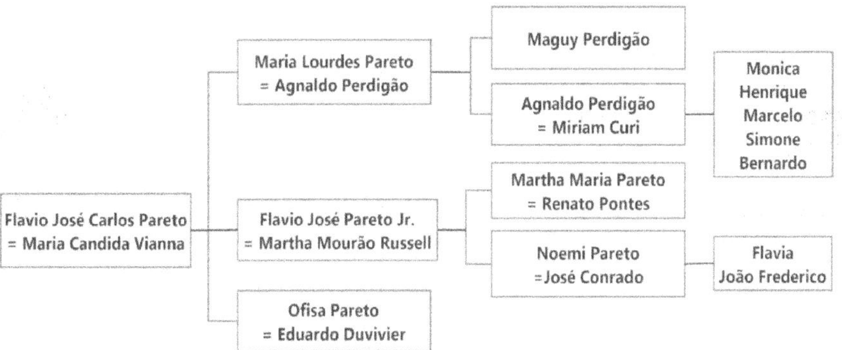

Figure 9 - Descendants of Flavio José Pareto

E. Afranio Pareto was born on 26 March (or May) of 1985 (or 1986) in Macaé. He died on 13 April 1887 from measles.

F. José Pareto, born on 8 October 1887 in Macaé. He died on 25 May 1889 from yellow fever.

G. Andrea Sophia Pareto was born on 13 Nov 1889 in Macaé. She married Clodomiro Vieira de Souza. Parents of a daughter:
    a. Marina de Souza married the physician Mario Alvarenga without children.

H. Ophisa Pareto born on 24 Jul 1893. She died while still an infant.

I. Raul Carlos Pareto (twin) was born on 15 September 1895 at Rua Real Grandeza 44, in Rio de Janeiro. He was studying in England in 1914 and joined the British army. He returned to Brazil due to the Spanish flu epidemic. Married to Euridice Tinoco (tia Tutinha). Parents of:
    a. Maria José Pareto (Zezé), born in 1818. She managed a school for poor children in the favela Dona Marta. She married Sidney Miller, who died of a lung issue. Parents of:
        i. Maria Lucia Miller was born in 1943. Married to José Paulo de Barros Duarte. Parents of:
            1. Maria de Fátima Duarte was born on 1st January 1969 in Rio. Journalist. Married to Erik Jean-Claude Bosch. After their children were born, they moved to France (Meaux). Parents of:
                a. Natasha Bosch was born on 27 April 1988 in Rio,
                b. Gabriel Bosch was born on 12 August 1991 in Rio.
            2. Fernando Antonio Duarte, designer of animated cartoons. Married to Erica.
            3. Maria Paula Duarte, Ph.D. in anthropology. Married to Antonio

Caccavari, Italian. They live in Crotone, Italy.

ii. Sidney Miller. Music composer. He died in 1980 from heart failure. Married Jeanne Marie Costa Ribeiro. Parents of:

1. Joana Miller, Ph.D. in anthropology.
2. Carlos Miller, photographer.

iii. Maria Aparecida Miller. Married Luiz Eduardo Tavares de Macedo, who worked in a Petrobras oil rig. Parents of:

1. Tomas Tavares de Macedo, industrial designer. Born on 11 December 1984 in Rio.
2. Lucas Tavares de Macedo, born in Rio.
3. João Tavares de Macedo, born on 24 November 1989.

iv. Bernardo Miller, professor. Married. Father of:

1. João Francisco Miller.

b. Raul Carlos Pareto Junior. Married to Vera de Oliveira. Parents of:

i. Luiz Cláudio Pareto, died in 1962.
ii. Adriana Pareto, married to Caetano de Sicco. Parents of:

1. Claudio de Sicco
2. Fabio de Sicco
3. Rodrigo de Sicco

c. Pedro Paulo Pareto was born in 1926. He died in 1988 in Petrópolis. He was married to Adalgisa Myriam de Souza. Parents of:

i. Pedro Paulo Pareto Jr. Married to Jomara Tadea Ribeiro. Parents of:

1. Gabriela Maia Pareto, born in 1992.
2. Rafaela Maia Pareto, born in 1995.

ii. Pedro Miguel Pareto[54], born 1961, married to Margarida Santos. Parents of:

---

[54] The only male descendants of Victorio Emmanuel, the patriarch, who may carry on the surname Pareto in Brazil are the two boys of Pedro Miguel Pareto (Rodrigo and João Pedro). Although this may still change,

1. Rodrigo Santos Pareto, born on 15 September 1998.
2. João Pedro Santos Pareto, born on 2 July 2003.
iii. Paula Beatriz Pareto.

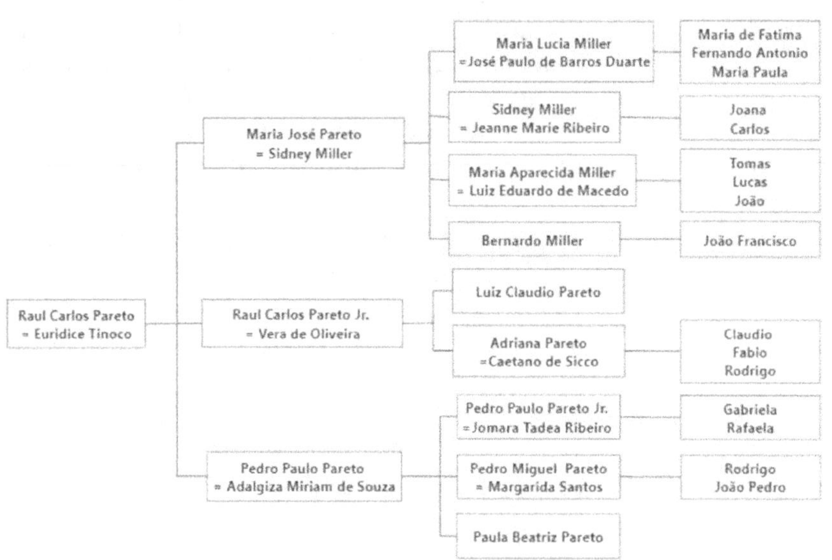

Figure 10 - Descendants of Raul Carlos Pareto

J. Carlos Raul Pareto (twin of Raul Carlos Pareto) was born on 15 September 1895. He married Esther Meyer in 1918. Parents of a daughter:

   a. Dulce Sophia Pareto was born in 1920. She died in 1944, single.

currently the only other continuous male line is the one of Vittorio Emmanuel Pareto (through his male grandsons Alexander, Henry and Gianluca), neither of whom live in Brazil. All the other lines end with female descendants, which cannnot carry further Pareto as their main surname.

The other children of Victorio Emmanuel

Francisca da Gloria, the third child of Victorio Emmanuel and
Maria da Gloria, was born on 25 July 1846 in Rio and was
baptized at the Church of Santissimo Sacramento[55]. She was
married to a Torres[56] and had two sons:
   A. Victorio Pareto Torres,
   B. Oscar Pareto Torres, engineer.

Francisca died on 7 Oct 1908 in Niteroi (RJ). She was buried with
her father and her brother João Victorio at the cemetery of São
João Batista in Rio.

**Maria da Gloria Pareto,
Frederico Ernesto Pareto, and
Victorio Emmanuel Pareto Junior.**

Not much is known about the three youngest children of Victorio
Emmanuel, all born in Macaé. When their mother, Maria da Gloria
died (1893), they were still living in the coffee plantation[57] of their
father in Concelção do Mabacu, fifth district of Macaé.

Maria da Gloria died on 2 Oct 1930 in Cruzeiro, São Paulo. Single.

Frederico Ernesto and Victorio Emmanuel also remained single and
continued living in Macaé. Frederico Ernesto was known to be
alive in 1904 but, by 1919, had already died. Victorio Emmanuel Jr
was still alive and living in Macaé in 1919.

[55] Register of Baptisms Book 1842-1847, pg 266v. Arquivo da Cúria
Metropolitana.
[56] Torres died before 1893.
[57] Fazenda Santo Agostinho.

About the author

Vittorio Emmanuel Pareto was born in 1937 in Rio de Janeiro, where he was raised, graduated in architecture, and married. He attended the renowned Tropical Course of the Architectural Association (London), returning to Brazil to participate in the new housing and planning program launched by the 1964 government.

Dr. Vittorio E. Pareto and Ugo (1919)

He returned to London in the mid-1970s, earning a Ph.D. in development planning from the University College London. In the early 1980s, he attended U.C. Berkeley as a post-graduate scholar. Following this, he was recruited by the United Nations Centre for Human Settlements (Habitat) in Nairobi to improve human conditions in underdeveloped regions. These activities led to a new independent consultancy career. He participated in numerous development projects in Latin America, Asia, Africa, and the Near East and designed structural plans for major cities and national capitals. His intense international activities and the rapid increase in criminality in Rio induced him to leave Brazil and settle in Aosta, Italy.

He took advantage of living in Italy to conduct genealogical research on the Pareto family, retrieving relevant primary data and joining genealogical and nobility associations. He retired from his professional activities in 2009 when he started writing on professional themes, family genealogy, and cooking, his preferred hobbies.

Vittorio Emmanuel has the inherited titles of marquis and patrician of Genoa. The Duke of Braganza, head of the Portuguese Royal House, honored him with the Grand Cross of the Order of St Michael of the Wing (Portugal), and King Kigali V of Rwanda with the Grand Cross of the Order of the Crown for his philanthropic activities in Africa.

Dr. Pareto is also a Commander of the Order of Christ and Counselor of the Three Orders of the House of Orleans and Bragança (Brazil), Knight of the Equestrian Order of Saint Sepulcher of Jerusalem (Holy See), and Order of the Saints Maurice and Lazarus (House of Savoy). He is a member of the Order of Vitéz (Hungary) and the Real Asociación de Hidalgos de España. The Italian government authorized him to use the title of **"*Cavaliere*"** (Knight) in Italy.

Vittorio Emmanuel married in 1959 and has three adult sons and five grandchildren. He and his wife live in the picturesque Alpine town of Aosta with Ugo, their lively mini pinscher.

Publications of Dr. V. E. Pareto

2013   - The Flagstad - story of a Nordic family.

2017   - The Urban Planning Papers.

2018   - The Pareto Project - genealogical research.

2019   - The Picorelli, a mémoire

2020   - The Brazilian Recipe Book.

2022   - Miguel de Carvalho

2022   - A Family Tale, the Pareto Story

2022   - The Cookbook

2023   - The Pareto Genealogical Records

All publications are available on Amazon.com

NOTES

www.ingramcontent.com/pod-product-compliance
Lightning Source LLC
Chambersburg PA
CBHW050708250726

48662CB00002B/902